W9-BFE-805

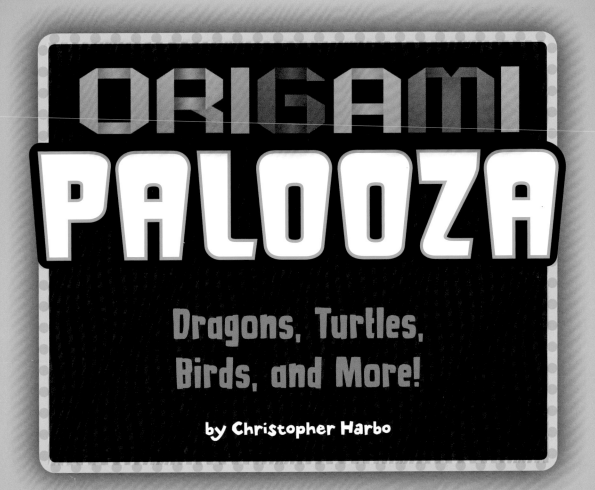

ORIGAMI PALOOZA

Dragons, Turtles, Birds, and More!

by Christopher Harbo

CAPSTONE PRESS

a capstone imprint

Edge Books are published by Capstone Press,
1710 Roe Crest Drive, North Mankato, Minnesota 56003
www.capstonepub.com

Library of Congress Cataloging-in-Publication Data
Harbo, Christopher L., author.
  Origami palooza : dragons, turtles, birds, and more! / by Christopher Harbo.
     pages cm.—(Edge books. Origami paperpalooza)
  Summary: "Provides instructions and photo-illustrated step diagrams for folding a variety
of traditional and original origami models"—Provided by publisher.
  Audience: Ages 8-14.
  Audience: Grades 4 to 6.
  Includes bibliographical references.
  ISBN 978-1-4914-2024-9 (library binding)
  ISBN 978-1-4914-2195-6 (eBook PDF)
1. Origami—Juvenile literature. 2. Handicraft—Juvenile literature. I. Title.
  TT872.5.H378 2015
  736.982—dc23   2014027877

Editorial Credits
Sarah Bennett, designer; Kathy McColley, layout artist; Katy LaVigne, production specialist;
Marcy Morin, scheduler

Photo Credits
All photographs done by Capstone Studio: Karon Dubke

Design Elements: Shutterstock: naihei

Printed in Canada.
102014   008478FRS15

Table of Contents

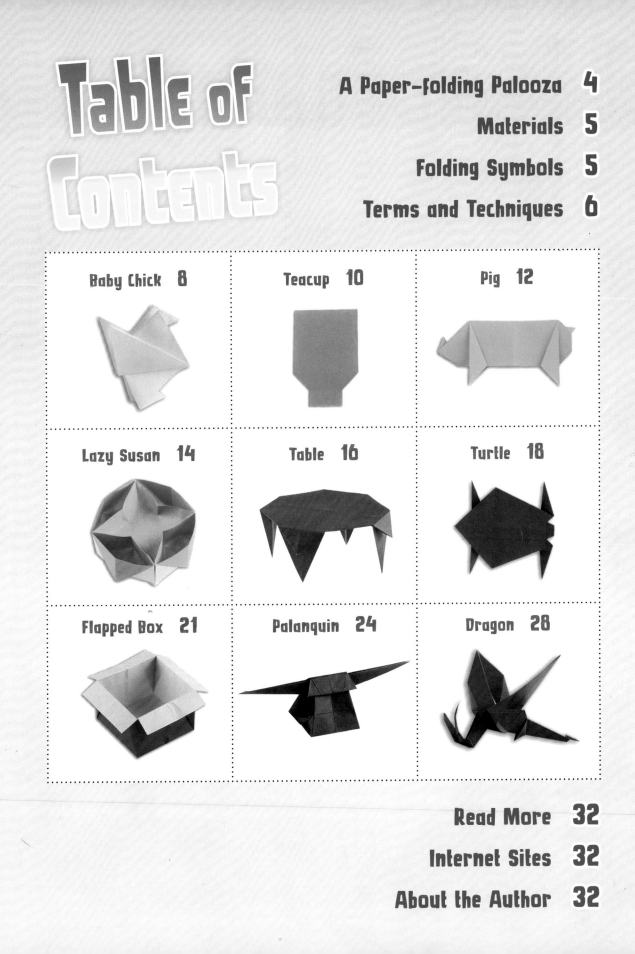

A Paper-Folding Palooza

Welcome to an origami extravaganza! Get ready to celebrate the Japanese art of paper folding with this remarkable collection of traditional and original origami models. Simple animals, such as the chick and the pig, will help you practice your folding skills. More complex models, such as the palanquin and the dragon, will amaze your friends and family. From turtles to teacups to lazy Susans, you'll discover that just about anything can be made from a single square of paper. What are you waiting for? Gather some paper and let's start folding. A paper-folding palooza awaits!

Materials

Origami is an affordable hobby because it doesn't require many materials to get started. In fact, you'll only need a square sheet of paper for most of the models in this book. A few models may require some extra materials, but you can easily find most of these items around the house:

Paper: While you can fold with just about any paper, authentic origami paper often works best. It is perfectly square, easy to fold, and has a crispness that holds its creases well. You'll find packets of origami paper with many fun colors, patterns, and sizes at most craft stores.

Scissors: Sometimes a model needs a snip here or there to pull off a key detail. You won't need it often, but keep a pair of scissors handy.

Ruler: Some models use measurements to complete. A ruler will help you measure.

Paper Trimmer: A good quality paper trimmer will come in handy when you want to cut paper to a custom size. Rotary blade paper trimmers are a good choice for precise, clean cutting. A variety of paper trimmers can be found at any craft store.

Pencil: Use a pencil when you need to mark a spot with the ruler.

Craft Supplies: Markers and other craft supplies will help you decorate your finished models.

Folding Symbols

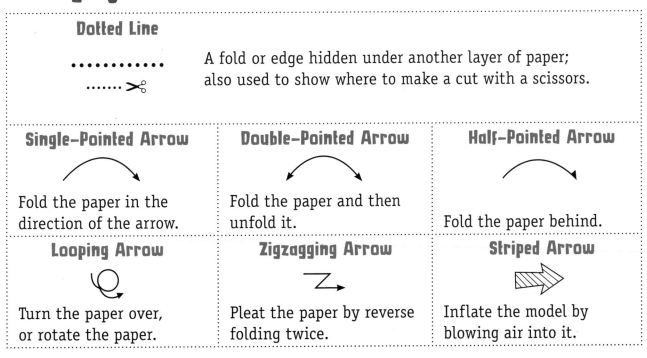

Dotted Line

A fold or edge hidden under another layer of paper; also used to show where to make a cut with a scissors.

Single-Pointed Arrow

Fold the paper in the direction of the arrow.

Double-Pointed Arrow

Fold the paper and then unfold it.

Half-Pointed Arrow

Fold the paper behind.

Looping Arrow

Turn the paper over, or rotate the paper.

Zigzagging Arrow

Pleat the paper by reverse folding twice.

Striped Arrow

Inflate the model by blowing air into it.

Terms and Techniques

Folding paper is easier when you understand basic origami folding terms and techniques. Practice the folds below before trying the models in this book. Bookmark these pages so you can refer back to them if you get stuck on a tricky step.

Valley folds are represented by a dashed line. One side of the paper is folded against the other like a book.

Mountain folds are represented by a dashed and dotted line. The paper is folded sharply behind the model.

Squash folds are formed by lifting one edge of a pocket. The pocket gets folded again so the spine gets flattened. The existing fold lines become new edges.

Inside reverse folds are made by opening a pocket slightly. Then you fold the model inside itself along the fold lines or existing creases.

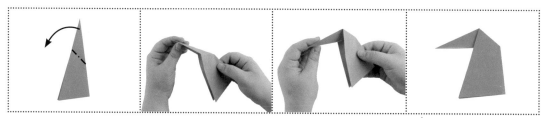

Outside reverse folds are made by opening a pocket slightly. Then you fold the model outside itself along the fold lines or existing creases.

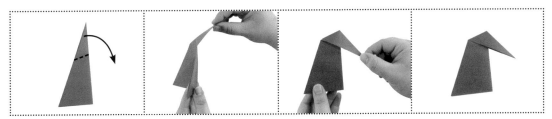

Rabbit ear folds are formed by bringing two edges of a point together using existing fold lines. The new point is folded to one side.

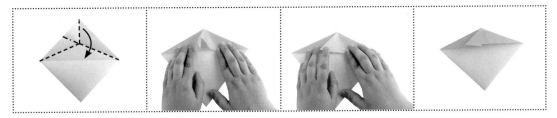

Petal folds are made by pulling a point upward and allowing its sides to come together as the paper flattens.

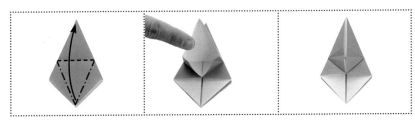

Pleat folds are made by using both a mountain fold and a valley fold.

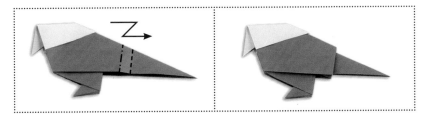

Mark folds are light folds used to make reference creases for a later step. Ideally a mark fold will not be seen in the finished model.

Baby Chick

♦ **Traditional**

Peep! Peep! Peep! With a few simple folds, this baby chick stands ready to test its new wings.

Tip: Try folding a whole brood of baby chicks using 3-inch (7.6-centimeter) squares.

1

Valley fold corner to corner.

2

Valley fold the left and right points to the bottom corner.

3

Mountain fold the model in half.

4

Valley fold the top layer. Repeat behind.

5

Inside reverse fold the top point to make a beak.

6

Inside reverse fold the bottom point to make feet.

7

Finished baby chick.

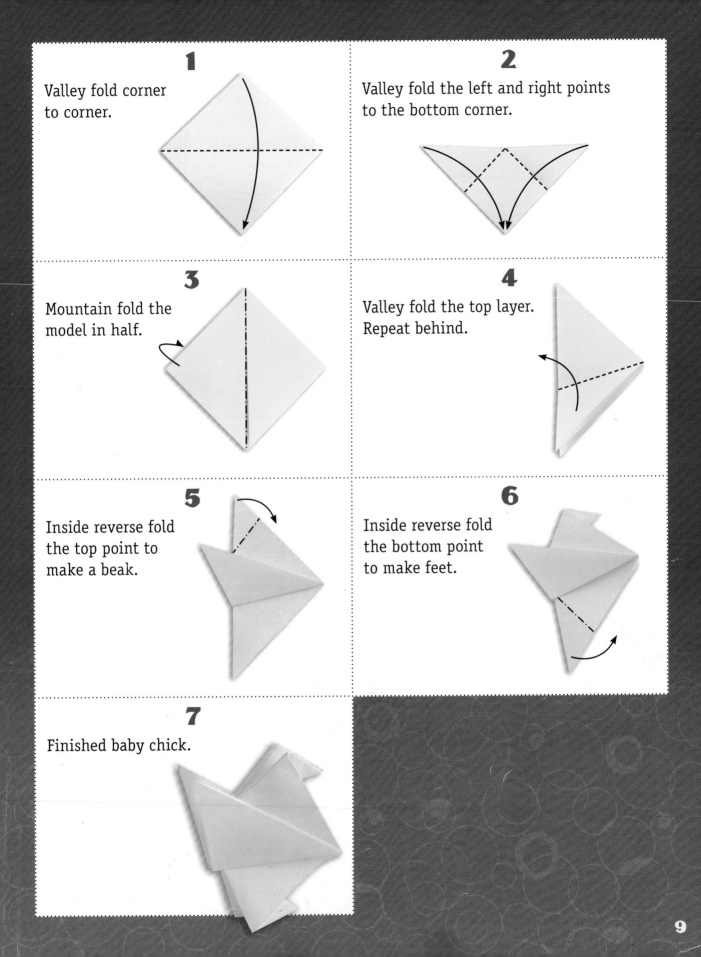

Teacup ◆ Traditional

Tea plays an important role in Japanese culture. This model represents the simple beauty of a traditional teacup.

1

Valley fold from edge to edge and unfold.

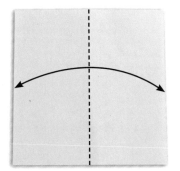

2

Valley fold the edges to the center.

3

Valley fold the corners to the center. Turn the model over.

4

Valley fold the point. Turn the model over.

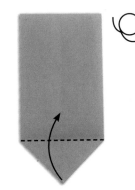

5

Valley fold the corners to the center. Turn the model over.

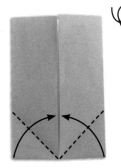

6

Squash fold by pulling the top point down.

7

Finished teacup.

Tip: Use textured, handmade paper to make your paper teacup look more like stoneware or pottery.

Pig ◆ Traditional

Who says pigs only look pretty in pink? With its little snout and tail, this paper porker couldn't get much cuter.

1

Valley fold edge to edge in both directions and unfold.

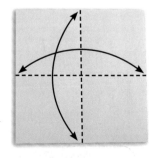

2

Valley fold the edges to the center.

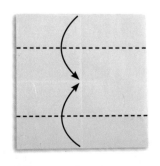

3

Valley fold the edges to the center and unfold.

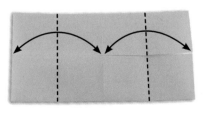

4

Valley fold the corners to the creases made in step 3 and unfold.

5

Squash fold the corners on the existing creases.

6

Mountain fold the model in half.

7

Valley fold the inside points to the vertical creases. Repeat behind.

8

Inside reverse fold the point to start the tail.

9

Inside reverse fold the hidden point to make the tip of the tail.

10

Mountain fold the top layer of the point to round the rump. Repeat behind.

11

Inside reverse fold the point to make the snout.

12

Finished pig.

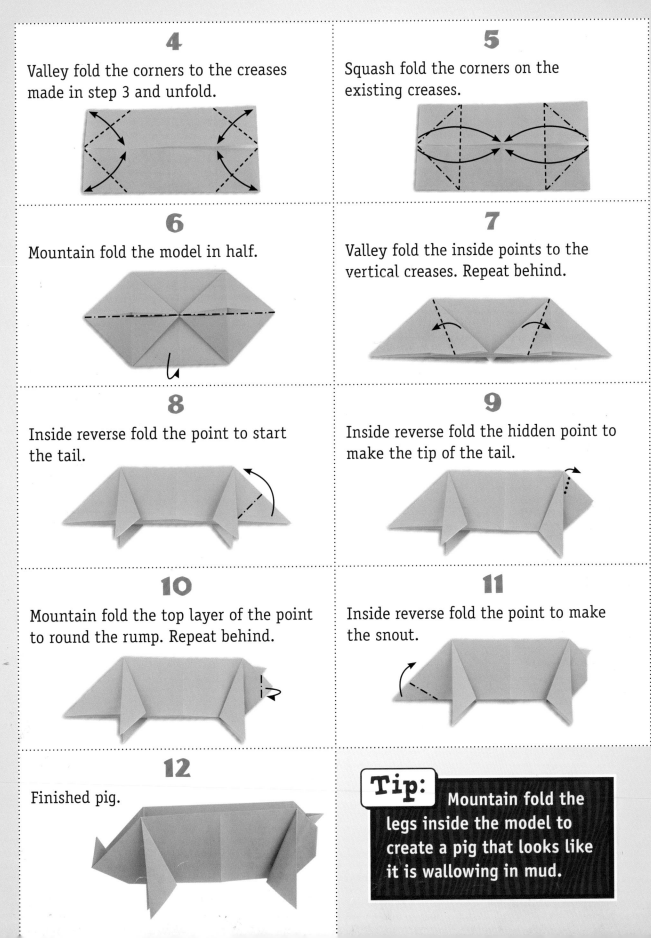

Tip: Mountain fold the legs inside the model to create a pig that looks like it is wallowing in mud.

Lazy Susan ◆ Traditional

This handy container takes its name from spinning serving trays—but there's nothing lazy about it. It provides five compartments to hold a variety of goodies.

Tip: Try using thicker paper to fold your lazy Susan. The finished container will have stiffer sides to hold heavier items.

1	**2**	**3**
Valley fold edge to edge in both directions and unfold. Turn the paper over.	Valley fold corner to corner in both directions and unfold. Turn the paper over.	Valley fold the corners to the center.

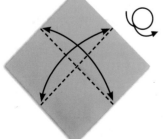

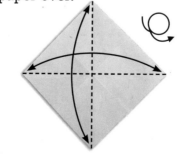

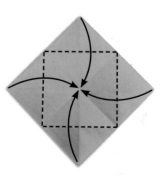

4

Valley fold the center corners to the edges.

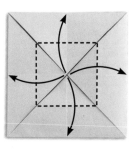

5

Turn the model over.

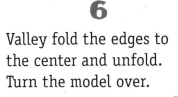

6

Valley fold the edges to the center and unfold. Turn the model over.

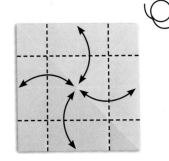

7

Push the center and mountain fold the sides on the creases to collapse the model.

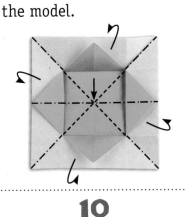

8

View of collapsing model in mid-step.

9

Inside reverse fold the top flaps. Repeat behind.

10

Push the bottom edges to separate the layers and round the model.

11

View of shaping the model in mid-step.

12

Finished lazy Susan.

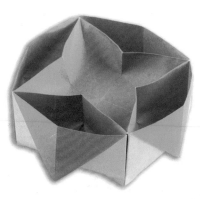

Table ◆ Traditional

Do you need a table for your action figures? If so, this is the ultimate "folding table" for you.

Tip: Try folding this model with a 3-inch (7.6-cm) square piece of paper. It can serve as a stool for a table made from a 6-inch (15-cm) square.

1

Valley fold corner to corner in both directions and unfold.

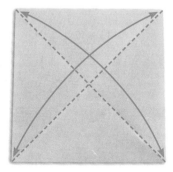

2

Valley fold the corners to the center and unfold.

3

Valley fold the edges to the center.

4

Valley fold the edges to the center.

5

Pull out the hidden corners under the top layer of paper.

6

Squash fold all four points.

7

Valley fold the edges of each of the four squares to their center creases and unfold.

8

Petal fold each of the four squares by using the creases made in step 7.

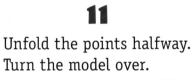

9

Valley fold the points to the center.

10

Valley fold the corners.

11

Unfold the points halfway. Turn the model over.

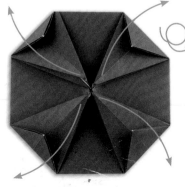

12

Finished table.

Turtle ◆ Traditional

As soon as they hatch, baby sea turtles scamper across the beach and into the ocean. Fold dozens of tiny turtles to create your own race to the waves.

Tip: The turtle's flat shape makes it an excellent choice for a gift tag on a present or a place card on a table.

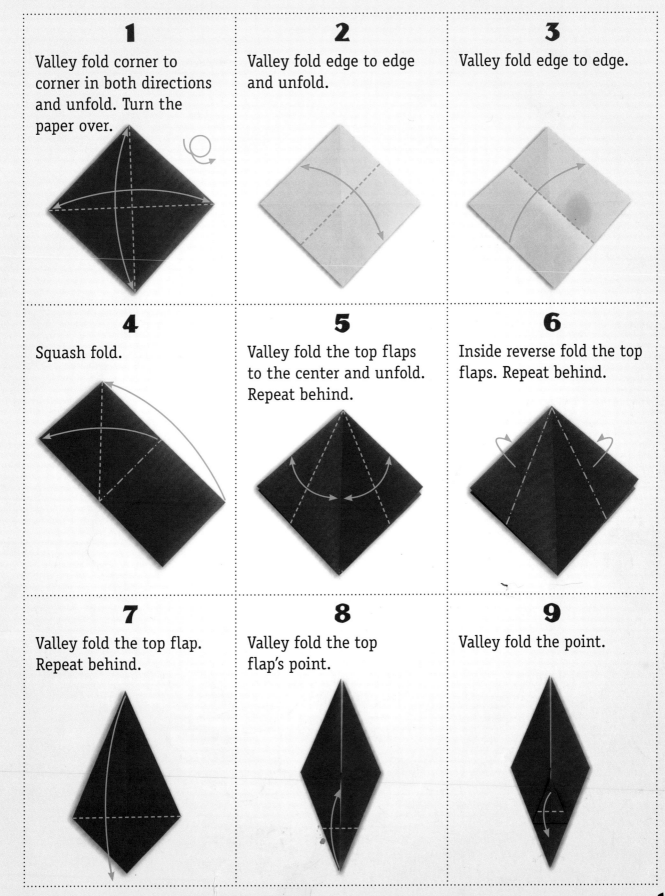

1

Valley fold corner to corner in both directions and unfold. Turn the paper over.

2

Valley fold edge to edge and unfold.

3

Valley fold edge to edge.

4

Squash fold.

5

Valley fold the top flaps to the center and unfold. Repeat behind.

6

Inside reverse fold the top flaps. Repeat behind.

7

Valley fold the top flap. Repeat behind.

8

Valley fold the top flap's point.

9

Valley fold the point.

10
Valley fold the point.

11
Valley fold the top flap on the existing crease.

12
Inside reverse fold the top points to make front legs.

13
Turn the model over.

14
Valley fold the top flap on the existing crease.

15
Valley fold the top flap.

16
Cut the top flap's point in half. Valley fold the two flaps to create the back legs. Turn the model over.

17
Finished turtle.

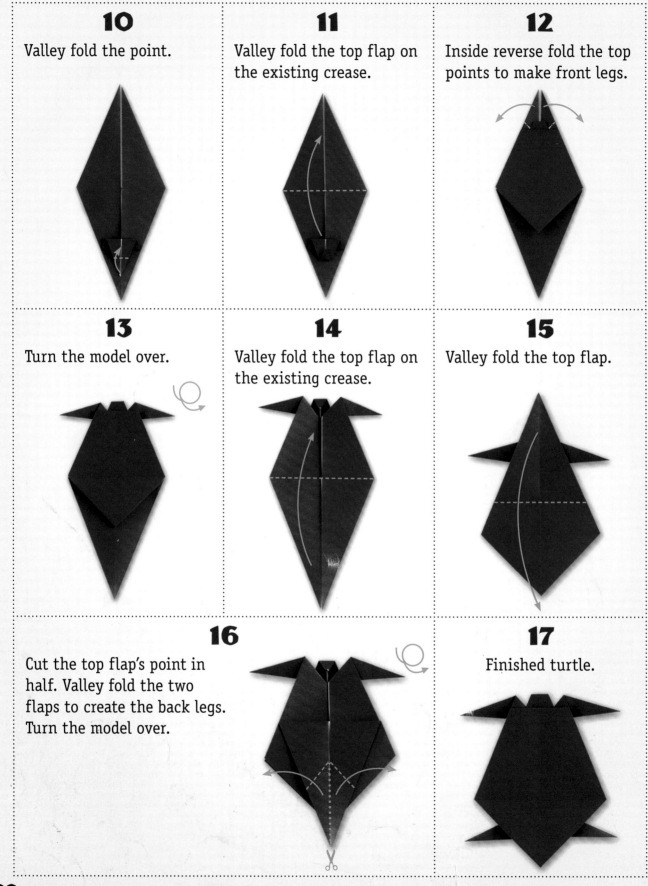

Flapped Box ◆ Traditional

The flapped box looks like an open packing box. It may not be fancy, but its deep walls will hold a ton of loot.

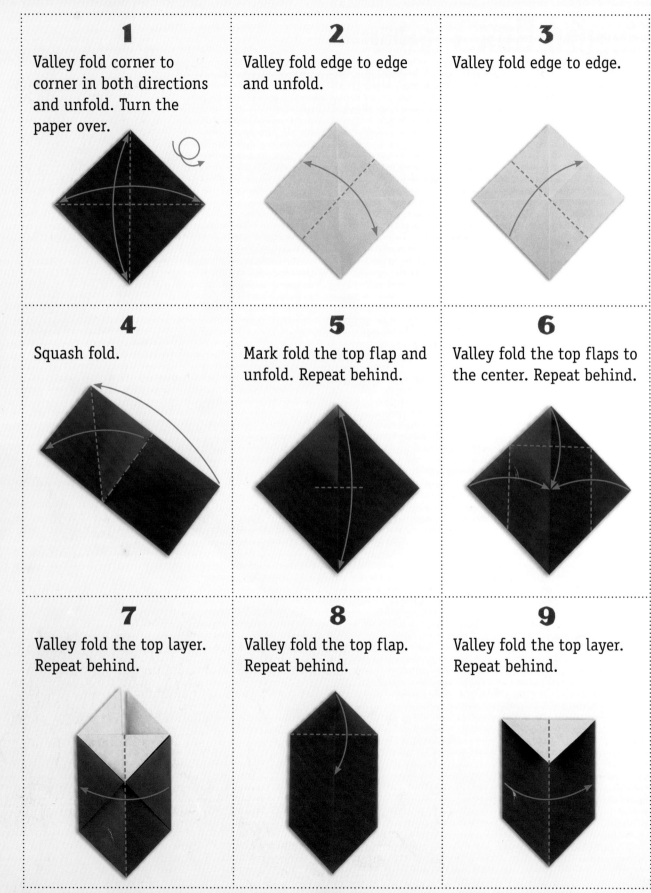

1

Valley fold corner to corner in both directions and unfold. Turn the paper over.

2

Valley fold edge to edge and unfold.

3

Valley fold edge to edge.

4

Squash fold.

5

Mark fold the top flap and unfold. Repeat behind.

6

Valley fold the top flaps to the center. Repeat behind.

7

Valley fold the top layer. Repeat behind.

8

Valley fold the top flap. Repeat behind.

9

Valley fold the top layer. Repeat behind.

10

Squash fold the inside corners. Repeat behind.

11

Mountain fold the top flaps. Repeat behind.

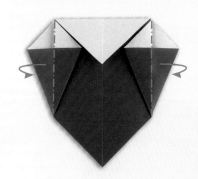

12

Valley fold the top flap as far as it will go. Repeat behind.

13

Valley fold the top layer. Repeat behind.

14

Repeat step 12 on the remaining two flaps.

15

Valley fold the bottom point and unfold.

16

Gently open the model and flatten the bottom.

17

Finished flapped box.

Tip:

Use thick paper with contrasting colors on each side to make your box stronger and more colorful.

Palanquin ◆ Traditional

Palanquins were once used to transport people throughout Asia. Their horizontal poles allowed palanquin bearers to carry passengers wherever they wished to go.

Tip: Try filling the inside of the palanquin with jellybeans or chocolate candies. It makes a great gift for a friend.

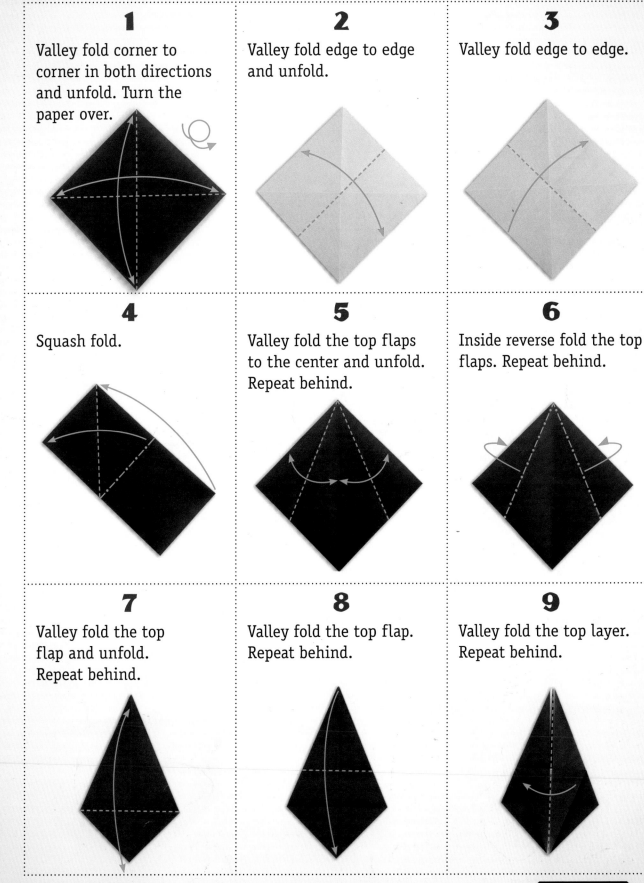

1
Valley fold corner to corner in both directions and unfold. Turn the paper over.

2
Valley fold edge to edge and unfold.

3
Valley fold edge to edge.

4
Squash fold.

5
Valley fold the top flaps to the center and unfold. Repeat behind.

6
Inside reverse fold the top flaps. Repeat behind.

7
Valley fold the top flap and unfold. Repeat behind.

8
Valley fold the top flap. Repeat behind.

9
Valley fold the top layer. Repeat behind.

Continued ➡

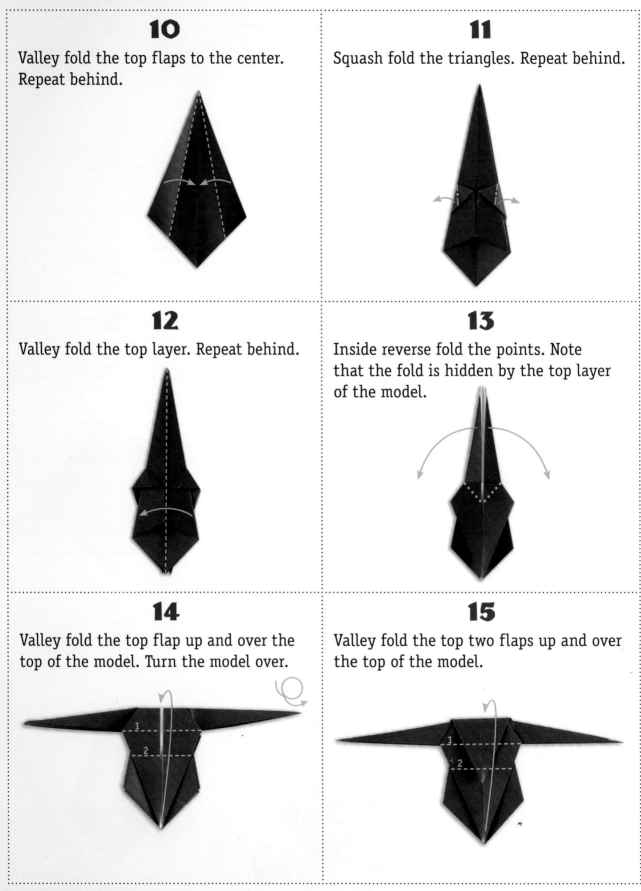

10

Valley fold the top flaps to the center. Repeat behind.

11

Squash fold the triangles. Repeat behind.

12

Valley fold the top layer. Repeat behind.

13

Inside reverse fold the points. Note that the fold is hidden by the top layer of the model.

14

Valley fold the top flap up and over the top of the model. Turn the model over.

15

Valley fold the top two flaps up and over the top of the model.

16

Turn the model over.

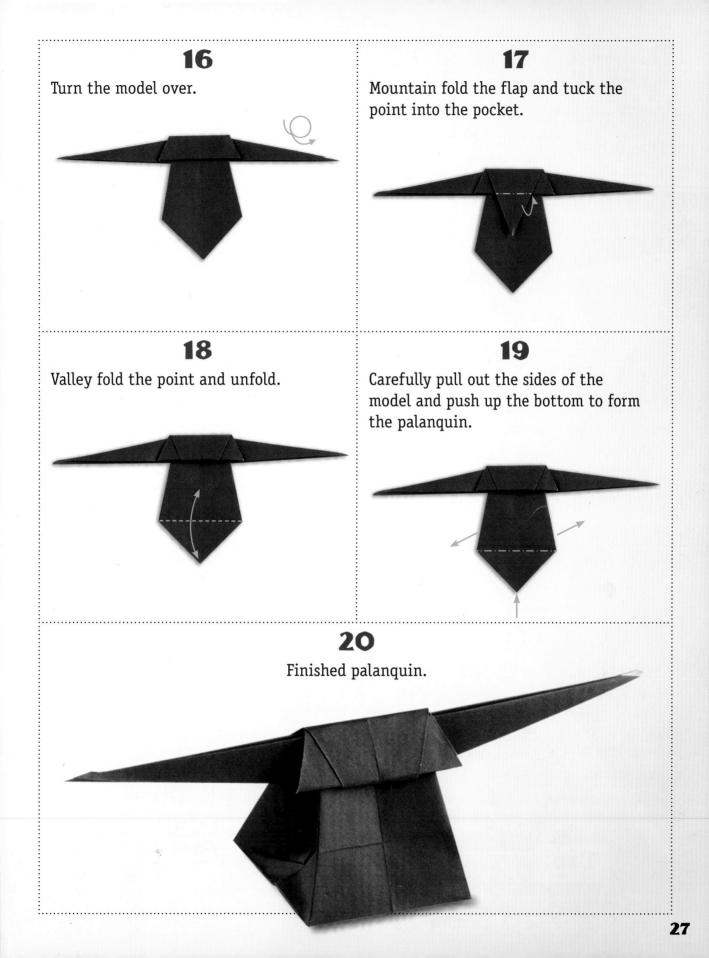

17

Mountain fold the flap and tuck the point into the pocket.

18

Valley fold the point and unfold.

19

Carefully pull out the sides of the model and push up the bottom to form the palanquin.

20

Finished palanquin.

Dragon ◆ Traditional model adpated by Christopher Harbo

Get ready to take your paper folding skills to new heights!
This origami dragon has spread its wings and is ready to soar.

Tip: Use a scissors to cut a small notch in the tail just behind the feet. Use the notch to perch your dragon on the edge of a glass or other thin object.

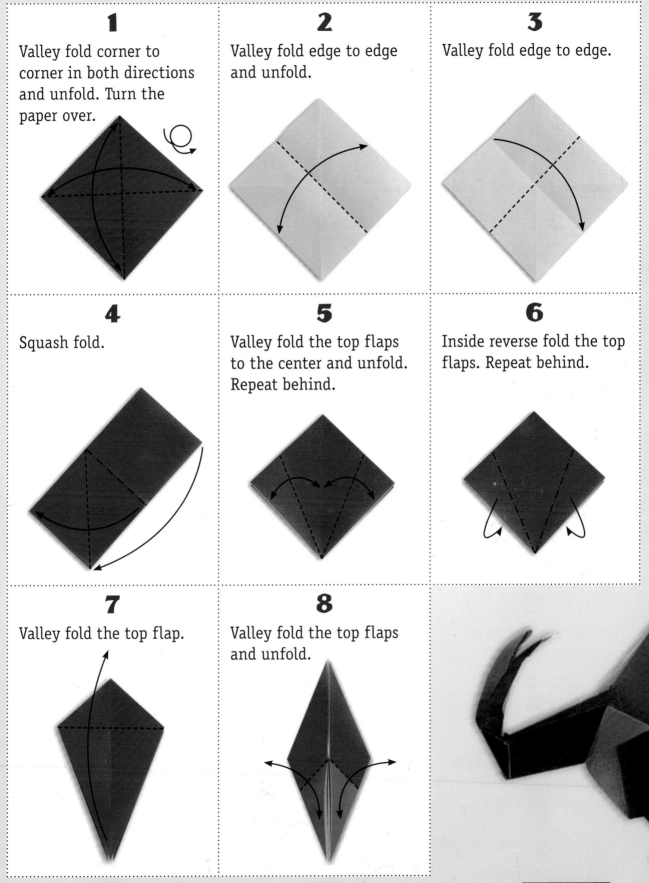

1

Valley fold corner to corner in both directions and unfold. Turn the paper over.

2

Valley fold edge to edge and unfold.

3

Valley fold edge to edge.

4

Squash fold.

5

Valley fold the top flaps to the center and unfold. Repeat behind.

6

Inside reverse fold the top flaps. Repeat behind.

7

Valley fold the top flap.

8

Valley fold the top flaps and unfold.

Continued ➡

9

Pull the flaps upward using the existing creases. Allow the flaps to open under the top layer.

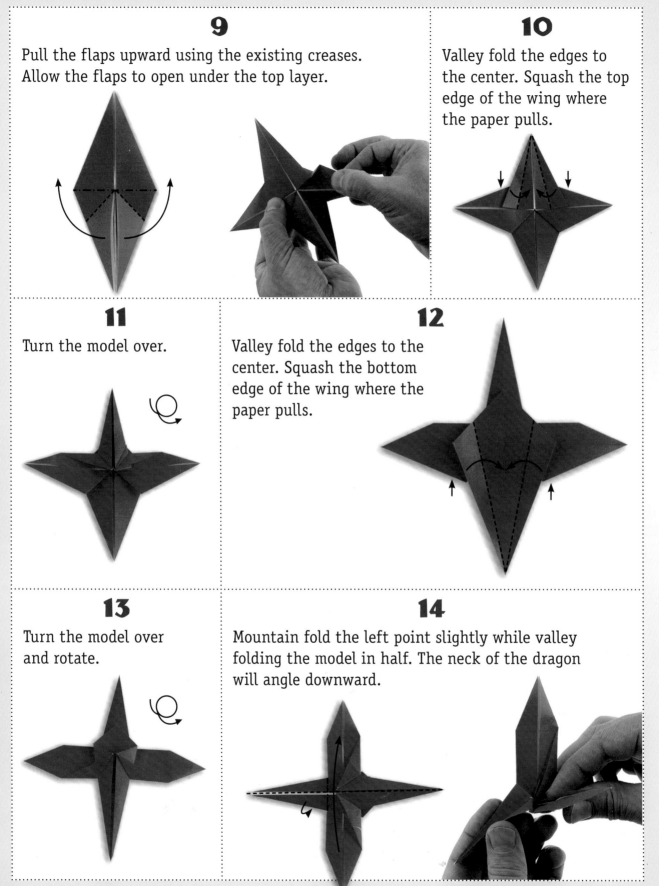

10

Valley fold the edges to the center. Squash the top edge of the wing where the paper pulls.

11

Turn the model over.

12

Valley fold the edges to the center. Squash the bottom edge of the wing where the paper pulls.

13

Turn the model over and rotate.

14

Mountain fold the left point slightly while valley folding the model in half. The neck of the dragon will angle downward.

15

Inside reverse fold the point to create a horn.

16

Valley fold the top layer to create a head. Repeat behind.

17

Outside reverse fold the small triangle to create feet.

18

Pleat the tail.

19

Cut the horn in half to make two horns. Curl each horn outward.

20

Push your fingers into the pockets under the wings to pull them down slightly.

21

Finished dragon.

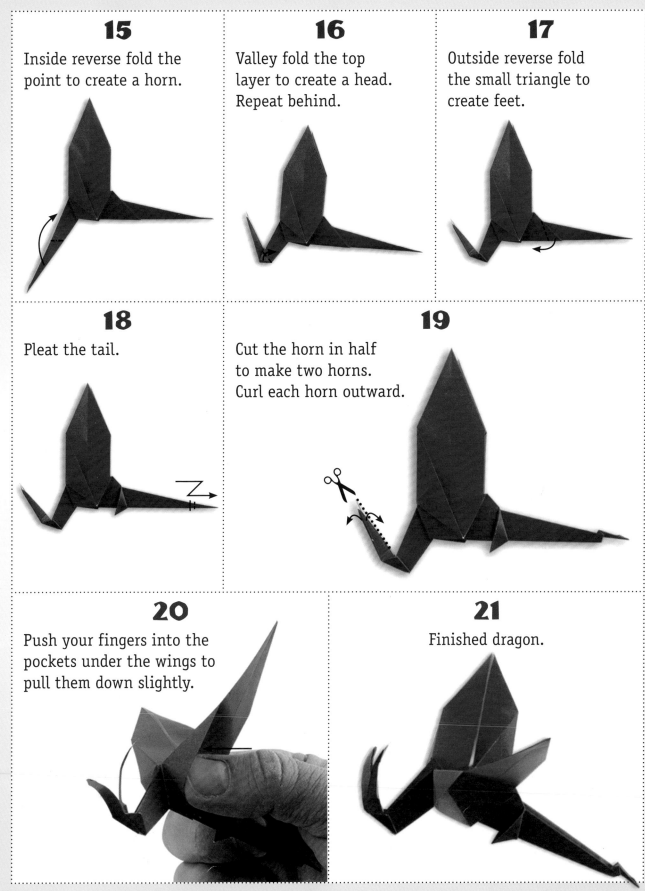

Read More

Bolitho, Mark. *Fold Your Own Origami Air Force*. Origami Army.
New York: PowerKids Press, 2014.

Miles, Lisa. *Origami Sea Creatures*. Amazing Origami.
New York: Gareth Stevens Publishing, 2014.

Owen, Ruth. *Halloween Origami*. Holiday Origami.
New York: PowerKids Press, 2013.

Internet Sites

FactHound offers a safe, fun way to find Internet sites related to this book. All of the sites on FactHound have been researched by our staff.

Here's all you do:
Visit *www.facthound.com*
Type in this code: 9781491420249

Check out projects, games and lots more at
www.capstonekids.com

About the Author

Christopher Harbo has a passion for origami. He began folding paper 10 years ago when he tried making a simple model for his nephews. With that first successful creation, he quickly became hooked on the art form. He ran to his local library and checked out every origami book he could find to increase his folding skills. Today he continues to develop his origami skills and loves the thrill of folding new creations. In addition to traditional origami and its many uses, he also enjoys folding paper airplanes and modular origami. When he's not folding paper, Christopher spends his free time reading Japanese manga and watching movies.